Dalton Brothers

Student Workbook

Chris Fife

© 12/30/14

Table of Contents

Dalton Brothers

Book One: The Promise

Student Study Guide

Introduction

Dalton Brothers: The Promise is book one of a seven book series following the Dalton brothers as they travel around the world in many adventures. The main purpose of the Dalton brother's series is to teach about geography in a fun way. Imagine taking a trip around the world with your friends or brothers and sisters. While the book is fictional and the characters are fictional the places and many of the things talked about in the book are real. While the book talks about the geography of North American focusing on Canada and the United States, the brothers only travel in the western area of both countries and by no means gives a complete and accurate picture of these areas.

The intent is for the reader to get excited about these places and do some investigation on her own. Real research is the discovery of the physical geography and the human geography of these places. There can be no substitute for actual travel and discovery of these places. First learn about these places then seek to visit them. Geography is about adventure, discovery, and excitement about learning new places and people around the world.

This student workbook has two parts a study guide for students to read the book and answer the questions. This helps students to study the material in the book and think about what they read about. The second part to the workbook is added material for North America including vocabulary, physical features, and includes other questions and activities that will help you to learn more about the geography of the United States and Canada.

This is only the beginning of your study it does not replace things you may learn in class or the things you need to discover for yourself. You can have a lot of fun learning about the adventures of the Dalton brothers and then starting your own journey of discovery. It is important to not stop with the first book. You need to read all seven books to get a clear picture of the world geography and to be able to learn what happens to the Dalton brothers.

Dalton Brothers: The Promise
Chapters 1-5

1. Have you ever done something for someone that was challenging? What was it?

2. What can a thunderstorm represent?

3. What are Josh, Ben, and Alex like? How does their relationship compare and contrast with your relationship with your family?

4. What is Eden, Utah like?

5. Where are Josh's parents?

6. Who is Jennifer and what announcement does she give to the Dalton brothers?

7. Who was Tabby?

8. What promise did Josh's parents make to Tabby?

9. What promises have you made to people you care about? Why is it important to make promises?

10. Think of a time when you made a promise and what motivated you to fulfill that promise.

11. How have you coped with trials in your life?

12. How does each brother deal with their parent's death?

13. What is the relationship like between Josh and Ben?

14. What are the Dalton brothers grandparents like?

15. What did the Dalton brothers parents teach them while they were growing up?

16. What has your parents, grandparents, or other members of your family taught you that you like?

17. What did Tabby establish before she died? Why was this important to the family?

18. What is the plan Josh comes up with that all of the boys accept?

19. How does religion influence the lives of the brothers?

20. Describe Jennifer?

21. Describe someone you care about or admire.

22. What is the relationship like between Jennifer and Josh?

23. In order for the boys to continue with their studies of school what do they have to do while they are away from home?

24. What do you think home schooling would be like?

25. What do the brothers do to get in shape for their journey?

26. What have you done to prepare for something important in your life?

27. Why is Jennifer concerned about the brothers going into the mountains?

28. What happens on King's Peak? What is the weather like? What food do they eat?

29. Describe an outdoor experience you have had.

30. How does climbing King's Peak help the brothers prepare to climb Denali?

31. What did you like about chapters 1-5?

Dalton Brothers: The Promise
Chapters 6-10

1. Where do the brother's go to stay before they head up to Alaska?

2. What did Ben forget at home when they arrived at the airport?

3. Where did the brothers live before they moved to Utah? Why do they like living in small towns? What are some benefits of living in a small town?

4. What looked like islands as the brothers flew into the state of Washington?

5. What did Ben and Alex do to Josh in Seattle as a joke?

6. What happened at the press conference? What did Jennifer, Ben, Alex, and Josh say to the press that got so much attention?

7. How would you feel if you had to give a speech to several reporters? What would you do if the reporters started to ask personal questions?

8. What is another name for Mt. McKinley?

9. Who was with Jennifer at base camp?

10. Who was the mountain guide they hired?

11. What did the brothers have to do before they were ready to climb the mountain?

12. What was their routine each day as they climbed the mountain?

13. Why would it be important to have a routine?

14. How did the weather impact their experience climbing the mountain?

15. What happened to Ben when he tried to climb too fast?

16. What secret did Heather have that she was going to tell John?

17. What does Alex do best?

18. What is Fairbanks like in the summer time?

19. Is there a North Pole Alaska?

20. What was the name of the road they traveled on through Canada?

21. What is the physical geography like in Canada?

22. What is the culture like in Canada?

23. What continued to bother them as they attempted to set up camp and eat dinner and breakfast?

24. What happened while they were on the road that forced them to stop riding on the road and set up their tent?

25. What wildlife did they see while they were traveling?

26. What happened at the hot springs?

27. What things would you like about biking and camping along the Alaskan Highway?

28. What are some things you would hate about traveling and camping along the Alaskan Highway?

29. What predictions can you make about what might happen to the brothers?

30. What motivations will keep them going? What would help make you continue to get up and travel day after day?

Dalton Brothers: The Promise
Chapters 11-16

1. What are the Canadian Rockies like?

2. What did the brothers not like about Jasper?

3. What happens to Josh in the Canadian Rockies?

4. What is the terrain like in Canada when the brothers get out of the mountains?

5. What do the brothers go and see in Calgary?

6. Describe Calgary.

7. Who did the brothers get to know in Canada? How did the people treat the brothers?

8. Describe Great Falls, Montana.

9. Why were there a lot of people in Great Falls cheering them on as they biked through the city?

10. Why was Josh worried about having a lot of people know where they were going? Why did he want to avoid the large cities?

11. What happened to their bikes in Yellowstone National Park?

12. Describe the area of Utah they traveled through.

13. What did the brothers do in Moab?

14. What was the story of the Hole in the Rock group of pioneers?

15. Where did the brothers spend the night after they left Bluff, Utah?

16. Why was Josh excited to be going to Albuquerque, New Mexico?

17. What was next to Alex and Ben as they took a nap in New Mexico?

18. Why didn't they spend the night in Farmington?

19. What would you have done if you were in the same situations as the Dalton Brothers?

20. How was geography important for the brothers to travel to the places they went to?

Vocabulary

Divide – a high point that determines the flow of water to the oceans

Aquaculture – fish farming

Fossil fuels – natural gas, petroleum, and coal non-renewable resources

Hurricane – ocean storms with wind speeds over 74 miles per hour

Great Plains (Prairie) – center of the continent, humid weather, treeless grasslands

Chinook – dry wind that blows in the Spring time on the eastern slopes of the Rockies

Marine West Coast – very wet climate located on the northwest coast of the United States including the states of Washington and Oregon. It extends into British Columbia in Canada.

Everglades – Wetland swamps in Florida that shelter a variety of plant and wildlife

Megalopolis – An area of dense population often including several large cities such as New York, Boston, and Philadelphia

Immigration – movement of people from one country to another country

Jazz – Type of music developed in the United States near New Orleans with a combination of European Harmonies and African rhythms

Province – political unit in Canada similar to a state in the United States

Parliament – the national legislature of Canada

Inuit – Arctic native people in Canada

Market Economies – allows people to own businesses

Wheat Belt – area of the Great Plains in the US and Canada that produces a lot of wheat

Corn Belt – area that grows a lot of corn from Ohio to Nebraska, and Quebec, Ontario, and Manitoba

Trans-Canada Highway – runs 4,860 miles from the west coast of Canada to the east coast.

Acid Rain- precipitation containing high amounts of acid material due to pollution

Eutrophication – over growth of algae in water that depletes oxygen killing other animals

Biographies

Sir John A. MacDonald (1867) - was the 1st prime minister in Canada was elected for six terms died in office

Stephen Harper- most recent prime minister of Canada was elected in 2006

Alexander Graham Bell (1847-1922) famous for inventing the telephone lived in Nova Scotia, Canada

Michael J. Fox – famous actor from Canada

Wayne Gretzky – famous hockey player from Canada

Celine Dion – famous singer from Canada

George Washington (1732-1799) general of the continental army that defeated the British in the revolutionary war and first president to the United States

Benjamin Franklin (1706-1790) founding father, inventor, writer, and scientist

Thomas Edison (1847-1931) – famous for invented a light bulb that would work

Henry Ford (1863-1947) – famous for production of automobiles in the United States

Mark Twain (1835-1910) – famous writer

Meriwether Lewis and William Clark – famous explorers of the American West

Physical Features

Mount McKinley (Denali) – the tallest mountain in North America located in Alaska 20,320 feet

Rocky Mountains – stretch from New Mexico to Alaska, tallest mountains in North America

Canadian Shield- east of the Canadian plains, subarctic climate coniferous forests

Appalachian Mountains – extend from Canada in the east to Alabama

Mississippi River – longest and most important river in the United States, one of the world's busiest waterways

Great Lakes – five lakes formed by glaciers contains a lot of fresh water, was very important for trasportation

Sunbelt – California, Arizona, and New Mexico noted for its mild climate and sunny days

Outsourcing – taking jobs and work to other locations to reduce business cost

Coastal Plain – Area of lowland in the south and southeast part of the United States including the states of North and South Carolina, Florida, Louisiana, Alabama, Mississippi, and Texas

Great Basin – area of basins and mountain ranges in Nevada and Utah

Columbia Plateau – plateau in the states of Washington, Oregon, and Idaho

Colorado Plateau – plateau in the states of Utah, Colorado, Arizona, and New Mexico

Missouri River – river in the west that flows to the Mississippi

Colorado River – river in Colorado that flows through Utah and Arizona to the Gulf of California

Mojave Desert – desert in California and Nevada

Sonora Desert – desert in Arizona

Hudson Bay – large bay in Canada that has a lot of transportation

St. Lawrence River – major transportation route in eastern Canada that flows from the Great Lakes

Grand Canyon – large canyon in Arizona

Niagra Falls – large falls in New York on the United States/Canadian border

Arches National Park – national park in Utah that has a lot of natural arches

Yellowstone National Park – national park in Idaho, Montana, and Wyoming that has a lot of wildlife and geysers is believed to be a super volcano

Mt. Saint Helens – volcano in the state of Washington that had a major eruption in May 1980

Major Cities

Ottawa – the capitol city of Canada. It is the fourth largest city with over a million people. It is said to be one of the cleanest cities in the world. It was founded in 1826.

Toronto – Canada's largest city with over 2 million people, it is located on Lake Ontario. The CN tower located in the city is one of the tallest manmade structures in the world.

Quebec City – has over 500,000 people. It is the capitol of the province of Quebec. It is located on the St. Lawrence River. It has a long French history.

Calgary – it is the third largest city in Canada with over a million people. It is the host of the largest rodeo in Canada the Calgary Stampede. It was also the host of the 1988 Winter Olympics.

Vancouver – west coast seaport in Canada with over 600,000 people

Washington D.C. – the capitol city of the United States have over 600,000 people with the commuters to work putting the population over a million during the workweek

New York – the largest city in the United States with over 8 million people, it is home to the Statue of Liberty a symbol of the United States. It is the financial center of the United States.

Chicago – Third largest city in the United States with over 2 million people, it is located on the coast of Lake Michigan in Illinois.

Los Angeles – known as the city of angels, it is the second largest city in the United States with over three million people. It is in California which is the largest populated state in the United States

Great Falls – the city has over 50,000 residents located in Montana along the Missouri river near a series of falls. Lewis and Clark had to portage around the falls on their way to the west coast.

Salt Lake City – the capitol and largest city of Utah with over 100,000 people. It is also the headquarters of the Church of Jesus Christ of Latter-day Saints (Mormons).

Albuquerque – it is the largest city of New Mexico with over 500,000 people

History

The history starts with the explorers. Leif Erickson was the first from Europe to explore North America landing in what is now Canada. Then there was John Smith who helped to establish the colony in Jamestown, and the Pilgrims at Plymouth Rock. But there were already hundreds of nations of American Indians already living in the Americas. These American Indians were decimated by disease and the European settlers forcing them from their land. Both Canada and the United States which were just colonies were built up in the east between 1600 and 1800. Spain, France, and Great Britain had claims of land in the southwest, northwest, and Mississippi area.

After independence the United States started to expand to the west. In 1805 Lewis and Clark went on their trip to the west exploring the Louisiana territory acquired from France. This opened up the west. In Canada fur trappers had already started to explore the west. On the west coast, Britain, France, and Russia were setting up settlements in the north and Spain in the south. Between 1805 and 1850 thousands of pioneers settled in the west including those heading to California with the gold rush of 1849, the Mormon pioneers, and those heading to the Oregon territory. After the civil war the transcontinental railroad connected the country from coast to coast increasing the population in the west in both the United States and Canada.

The United States and Canada share a similar history and geography. They both were settled by European nations and had native people already living here. You will find the Rocky Mountains in Canada and the United States as well as the Great Plains. Both countries have British and French ties. Both countries are considered lands of opportunity and thousands of immigrants come to both countries seeking a better life.

The differences of Canada and the United States are that Canada has the Canadian Shield, parts of Canada are in the arctic circle the United States has deserts in the southwest and a tropical climate in Florida and Hawaii. The United States has strong ties to Mexico while Canada has strong ties to Great Britain and France. The United States has a president and Canada has a prime minister. Football is popular in the United States and hockey is popular in Canada. The United States has more than 300 million people and Canada has fewer than 40 million people.

Resources

Websites:

http://www.nationalgeographic.com/education

http://www.glencoe.com

http://www.canada.ca/en/index.html

http://us-keepexploring.canada.travel/

http://www.usa.gov/

Questions

Describe an influential person from the United States and one from Canada.

Describe two physical features in Canada and two in the United States.

Describe two major cities in Canada and two in the United States.

Briefly explain the history of North America.

Compare and contrast the United States and Canada

Problem Solving

How can the United States and Canada become more unified? What are some things that both countries could do to work with each other on? How can Canada help support the United States and how can the United States help to support Canada?

Make a list of some major concerns and challenges each country has, then figure out a plan how the countries could work together to overcome those challenges.

If a major natural disaster hit Canada how could the United States help them?

Activities

1. Students need to read the first book in the Dalton Brother's series and complete the study guide that goes with it.

2. Students need to read through the extra material in this workbook about North America and answer the questions that go with it.

3. Students need to complete the problem solving activities.

4. Students can do further research about the United States and Canada and write a paper about the history, geography, or current challenges each country is facing.

5. Students can work with a partner or in a group focusing either on Canada or on the United States. The groups or partners then take the information they learned and teach another group that took the other country. Once the groups have had a chance to talk about it they can then report what they learned to the class.

6. Students can put together posters with information and pictures on them from different states or provinces. Once they are completed they can share what they learned with the class.

7. Students can chose another fictional story that describes the geography of Canada or the United States and write a report on it.

Dalton Brothers

Book Two: Aconcagua

Student Study Guide

Introduction

Dalton Brothers: Aconcagua is book two in the Dalton Brother's series. It describes how the brothers travel through Latin America starting in New Mexico and traveling through Mexico. They go through Central America and South America to the tip of the continent and then make preparations to travel to Antarctica.

Two friends in real life traveled from Alaska to the tip of South America by bike. Only one of them made it. One died when he was hit by a car in a major city. The story was part of my inspiration for writing the Dalton Brothers series. There have been several people who have biked from Alaska to Argentina and many of them did it to support a cause like the Dalton brothers in the books. I even came across a family who biked from Alaska to Argentina.

The hardest part of the trip from Alaska to Argentina is in Latin America there is all kinds of dangers along the trail. The brothers have to contend with bandits, the weather, and even an erupting volcano. The road in Latin America is prone to earthquakes, volcanoes, adverse weather conditions, and unstable governments. It is amazing to just climb Denali and bike from Alaska to the United States. Now the brothers bike all of Latin America and climb Aconcagua the tallest mountain peak in the Andes the longest mountain range in the world. Aconcagua is an easier climb than Denali, but it can still be dangerous.

The Dalton brothers have to face a lot of their fears along the way. They also have to come to face the death of their parents as they climb the mountain that had killed their parents. The brothers finally start to grow closer together as Josh and Ben struggle with who should be in charge of the journey. The trip starts to take a heavy toll on their bodies as they bike hundreds of miles a day towards their goal of reaching Argentina. Since Argentina is in the southern hemisphere the brother's time reach it in December which is the start of their summer.

They also want to be in the perfect position to travel to Antarctica and go across it before the winter sets in and they are stuck on Antarctica. This part of their journal really tests their abilities and fortifies their convictions to finish the trip around the world and climbing the seven peaks on all of the continents.

Dalton Brothers: Aconcagua
Chapters 1-5

1. What did the brother's do in Albuquerque?

2. What was Jennifer's role?

3. Why was it important for the brothers to get to Argentina by December?

4. What was the boarder of Mexico like?

5. What is a Maquiladora?

6. Why were they afraid of drug cartels?

7. What are the people like in the small villages of Mexico?

8. What is the Cerro Con Caballo?

9. What do the brothers do when a truck attempts to run them off the road?

10. Why did the brothers help the men in the truck who attempted to run them over?

11. Who helped them get supplies?

12. What happened in Chihuahua?

13. How were the Aztecs conquered?

14. What is Guatemala like?

15. What are some problems the brothers have with humidity?

16. What is Honduras like?

17. What killed thousands of people in Honduras in 1998?

18. What happened in Tegucigalpa?

19. What happened in Nicaragua?

20. How did the brothers help the people of the village?

21. What would you do in an Earthquake?

Dalton Brothers: Aconcagua
Chapters 6-10

1. Why did the man at the boarder laugh?

2. What is Costa Rica the leading producer of?

3. What caused the earth to shake in Costa Rica?

4. Why did Josh have a panic attack?

5. What is Gallo Pinto?

6. What is San Jose like?

7. What trouble did the brothers get into at the border of Panama?

8. What US president got the Panama Canal built?

9.   What did they eat in Panama?

10. What almost knocked Alex off bike?

11. How long had the brothers been away from home when they reached South America?

12. Describe Columbia's history.

13. What did they accomplish while they were in Columbia?

14. What does Columbia produce 90% of?

15. What is Bogota like?

16. Who was Simon Bolivar?

17. What did they eat in Bogota?

18. What happened with the women in Columbia?

19. Why were the brothers arrested?

20. How did Ben help them escape from the police?

21. How did the brothers get out of Columbia?

22. What country did they have to go through to get to Peru?

23. What is Lima Like?

24. What is unique about Ecuador?

25. Where did Ben and Alex want to go?

26. What is Machu Picchu like?

27. What did Ben tell a woman at Machu Picchu?

28. What happened to Butch Cassidy and the Sundance kid?

Dalton Brothers: Aconcagua
Chapters 11-14

1. Describe the country of Chile.

2. Why were the brothers going to camp along the way through Chile?

3. How did Ben break his fingers?

4. What other troubles did they have in Chile?

5. What country is Aconcagua in?

6. Why is climbing Aconcagua so important for the brothers?

7. Why did they go to sleep laughing?

8. Describe Argentina.

9. How did they have to go to the bathroom on Aconcagua?

10. Why did Manuel want to help them as their guide?

11. How high is Plaza Argentina?

12. Why did they start drinking more water?

13. What is the name of the harder route up Aconcagua?

14. How high is camp one?

15. What did Josh teach Jennifer?

16. What did Manuel say about health care?

17. What did Victor blame himself for?

18. How high is camp two?

19. Where did they have to go before making it to the top?

20. What time did they get up to make a summit attempt?

21. What is Josh's favorite drink?

22. What did Jennifer and Josh say to each other?

23. Who was the first to see Santiago?

24. What did Josh write in his journal?

25. What would you have liked about traveling through South America?

26. Would you have climbed Aconcagua?

27. What do you think would have been the most difficult part of the journey?

Vocabulary

Andes – longest mountain range in the world, located in South America.

Altiplano – high plains in South America

Llanos – grasslands of Colombia and Venezuela

Pampas – grasslands of Argentina

Amazon River – largest river in South America the world's second largest river after the Nile

Tierra Helada – frozen land ranges from 12,000 to 16,000 feet

Tierra Fria – cold land ranges from 6,000 to 12,000 feet

Tierra Templada – temperate land ranges from 2,500 to 6,000 feet

Tierra Caliente – hot land ranges from sea level to 2,500 feet

Atacama Desert – along the coast of Chile the driest desert in the world

Mestizo – people of mix of European and Native American decent

Tenochtitlan – capitol city of the Aztecs which had chinampas or floating gardens

Hernan Cortes – defeated the Aztecs in 1521

Machu Picchu – Inca city built in the Andes

Maquiladoras – are along the US Mexican border, they are factories in a free trade zone

Deforestation – cutting down the trees in the forest

Biographies

Bartolomé de Las Casas (1484-1566) – he fought for the rights of the native peoples in Latin America helping those during the conquest.

Simón Bolívar (1783-1830) – he helped several countries become independent from Spain including the present-day countries of Columbia, Venezuela, Ecuador, Peru and Bolivia.

Diego Rivera (1886-1957) – Famous Mexican artist

Edison Arantes do Nascimento "Pelé" (1940-) – Considered the best soccer (Futbol) player of all time. He is from Brazil.

Rigoberta Menchú (1959 -) a native of Guatemala, she has been an advocate for native rights and won the 1992 Nobel Peace Prize

Ernesto "Che" Guevara (June 14, 1928 – October 9, 1967) – Gorilla fighter who helped in the Cuban revolution, and several others, he was captured and executed in Bolivia in 1967.

Physical Features

The Andes Mountains are the dominant physical feature of South America. They are what create the terrain and climates of South America. They consist of cordilleras which are mountain ranges that run parallel to each other. There are a few plateaus in Latin America including the altiplano in Peru and Bolivia. There is also the Mato Grosso Plateau and Brazilian Highlands located in Brazil.

The lowland regions have inland grasslands kwon at the Llanos in the north in Colombia and Venezuela. Then there is the pampas of Argentina and Uruguay. These areas are used for ranches and farms. The cowhands are known as gauchos. These areas produce a lot of wheat and corn.

The water system of South America is dominated by the Amazon River basin. Hundreds of small rivers join the Amazon which flows to the Atlantic Ocean. The rivers help to provide hydroelectric power.

Most of Latin America is based on the climate of the Andes. It is drier on the west coast with the Atacama Desert being the driest in the world. On the east side of the Andes it is very west and the rivers empty into the Amazon. The Amazon basin is tropical, the north part of South America is tropical and so is most of Central America.

Major Cities

Beunos Aires – capitol city of Argentina and one of the largest in Latin America

Santiago – capitol and largest city of Chile

Havana – capitol of Cuba

Mexico City – capitol of Mexico and one of the largest cities in the world

Lima – capitol of Peru

Rio de Janeiro – one of the largest in Brazil

Sal Paulo – the largest city in Latin America and one of the largest in the world located in Brazil

History

Latin America was dominated by European conquest. After Columbus arrived in 1492, the Spanish Conquistador Hernan Cortes defeated the Aztecs through making friends with their rivals and using germ warfare. The indigenous population could not compete with European weapons and diseases. Soon all of Latin America was controlled by a European country with Spain controlling most of Latin America. Portugal controlled Brazil and several countries had possession of territories in the Caribbean and Northern part of South America including France and England.

Spain brought with them a host of foods, animals, language, and religion. Many of the people from Spain also intermarried with the native population creating a middle class called Mestizo. In the early 1800s Mexico fought for its independence from Spain and finally accomplished it. Columbia, Bolivia, and Peru also became independent with Simon Bolivar helping those areas gain their independence from Spain. Since their independence most of the countries of South America have gone through civil war with one brutal dictator being replaced with another.

Today many Latin American countries face a lot of challenges with helping their people rise from poverty, overcome diseases, and building a strong infrastructure to support the future. Some of the countries still have troubles with gorilla groups and drug cartels. But many of them are getting better and working to help build their countries and help those in need of help.

Resources

Websites:

http://familyonbikes.org/blog/about-2/about/

http://mexicotoday.org/culture/family-bike-ride-through-all-mexico-and-more%E2%80%A6

http://www.businessinsider.com/what-its-like-to-ride-your-bike-20000-miles-from-alaska-to-argentina-2012-2?op=1

http://www.earthcycle.org/

Books:

Reid, Michael The Forgotten Continent: the battle for Latin America's soul. New Haven [Conn.] ; London : Yale University Press, c2007

Questions

What are two major cities in Latin America?

Describe two physical features in Latin America.

Describe the culture of Latin America.

Briefly explain the history of Latin America.

Compare and contrast the United States and Latin America

Problem Solving

How can Latin American countries have stronger governments? What are some things that the countries of Latin America do to work with each other? How could the United States help support the governments of Latin America?

Make a list of some major concerns and challenges each country has, then figure out a plan how the countries could work together to overcome those challenges.

If a major natural disaster hit in Latin America, how could the countries help each other?

Activities

1. Students need to read the second book in the Dalton Brother's series and complete the study guide that goes with it.

2. Students need to read through the extra material in this workbook about Latin America and answer the questions that go with it.

3. Students need to complete the problem solving activities.

4. Students can do further research about Latin America and write a paper about the history, geography, or current challenges each country is facing.

5. Students can work with a partner or in a group focusing either on one country in Latin America. The groups or partners then take the information they learned and teach another group that took a different country. Once the groups have had a chance to talk about it they can then report what they learned to the class.

6. Students can put together posters with information and pictures on them from different countries. Once they are completed they can share what they learned with the class.

7. Students can chose another fictional story that describes the geography of Latin America or the United States and write a report on it.

Dalton Brothers

Book Three: Antarctica

Student Study Guide

Introduction

Dalton Brothers: Antarctica is book three in the Dalton Brother's series. It describes how the brothers finish traveling to the tip of Argentina. They set sail on a sailboat where they head for Antarctica. In Antarctica their goals are to cross the continent and to climb the highest peak of Antarctica which is Vincent Massif. The mountain is not that tall compared to Ancacagua and Denali, but with the climate of Antarctica climbing any mountain proves to be a huge challenge.

The harshness of the weather proves to be too much for the brothers. They call in for help from a private company that provides support. Jennifer does her best to keep the brothers alive. Antarctica proves to be the last frontier where even the experts have trouble surviving. With the lowest recorded temperature and the highest speed winds Antarctica is the ultimate challenge.

The brothers grow closer together and find how they must rely on each other for support in order to be able to get to the other side of the world. This book refers to a real life adventure in Antarctica when Ernest Shackelton and his crew of the Endurance are trapped in Antarctica in the early 1900s with no hope for a rescue must survive for nearly two years in this harsh environment and rescue themselves. In what seemed impossible all of the members of the crew survived. It proved to be the most incredible story of survival in history.

Students as they read the book and do the activities can pretend they are either explorers like Ernest Shackelton attempting to travel across Antarctica or they can pretend they are scientists who have been asked to study something in Antarctica and will spend the arctic summer researching something.

Dalton Brothers: Antarctica
Chapters 1-5

1. Why were they worried about their trip ahead?

2. Why were they thinking about going home?

3. What did they decide to do?

4. How did the brothers help an older couple in Santiago?

5. Describe Tierra del Fuego?

6. What desert did they travel through?

7. What happened to Josh?

8. Why did they want Josh to jump on one foot?

9. How will the brothers get their food in Antarctica?

10. What happened to Ernest Shackelton and his men?

11. Why did the story of Ernest Shackelton haunt Ben?

12. Why were the days getting longer?

13. Where was the wealth of the countries in Latin America?

14. What did the brothers do with their bikes?

15. What did they do with the pictures they took?

16. What did Josh think was in the water off of South America?

17. Which of the brothers were scared of going in a boat?

18. What did Ben have a nightmare about?

19. What happened to their sailboat?

20. How did they get across the Straight of Magellan?

21. How did Josh want to get to Port Williams?

22. What did Ben remember about his father?

23. What did their raft look like?

24. What does the raft experience remind Alex of?

25. What was Josh thinking of most of their trip?

26. What made the hardships worth it?

27. What movie did they talk about?

28. Who fell off the raft?

Dalton Brothers: Antarctica
Chapters 6-10

1. What is Patagonia like?

2. What country did people immigrate from?

3. What is Brazil like?

4. What is Rio de Janero?

5. What was French Guiana used for?

6. What do they eat the most for breakfast?

7. What practical joke did Ben play on Josh?

8. What did they use to find Port Williams?

9. Why was it important for them to stay on their timetable?

10. What happened to them when they reached the beach?

11. What did they do to get warm after being in the cold water?

12. When did they arrive in the village to get help?

13. Who helped the brothers get to Port Williams?

14. Who showed up in Port Williams?

15. What was their sailboat like?

16. What was wrong with Ben and Jennifer?

17. What did Ben decide Jennifer should do?

18. What support did they decide to have in Antarctica?

19. What is the Southern tip of South America called?

20. What islands where they going to get supplies at?

21. What stars did they see that are part of the Southern Hemisphere?

22. How did Alex get back on the boat?

23. What where people wearing on Antarctica?

Dalton Brothers: Antarctica
Chapters 11-18

1. What was the name of the station they went to in Antarctica?

2. What did Alex see in the Ocean?

3. What was big business in the waters near Antarctica a century ago?

4. What were they afraid of running into?

5. What was SERCA?

6. What did they eat at the station?

7. Who is Jason Phillips?

8. What does Cody Mitchell do?

9. Who will sail the boat to the other side of Antarctica?

10. How many people live on Antarctica any given time of the year?

11. Who was the first to reach the South Pole?

12. How were they going to cross Antarctica?

13. What was Jennifer's experience being with the SERCA crew?

14. How did they go to the bathroom?

15. How did the SERCA crew spend their time in Antarctica?

16. How did they ski up the hills?

17. Why didn't Ben want to stay in a SERCA tent?

18. Describe Vinson Massif?

19. Who was filming the climb?

20. How many people have climbed Vinson Massif?

21. Why did Ben and Alex get Josh out of his sleeping bag?

22. What were the winds like on the mountain?

23. Why did they need to travel to the South Pole?

24. What was at McMurdo?

25. How did the SERCA team travel?

26. Who was the first to reach the South Pole?

27. What was the US station like?

28. Why were the brothers running out of food?

29. What were their thoughts like when they were running out of food?

30. How were they able to get food?

31. What did they find at Dumont?

32. What did Ben write about in his journal?

Vocabulary

Vinson Massif – tallest point in Antarctica at 16,066 ft

Antarctic Minke Whale – a whale near Antarctica that was hunted almost to extinction

Emperor Penguins – Penguins found in Antarctica the father holds the eggs off the ground until it hatches

Elephant Seal – a seal found in Antarctica

Biographies

Robert F. Scott made a failed attempt to reach the South Pole

Roald Amundsen was the first person to reach the South Pole

Admiral Richard E. Byrd was the first to fly over the South Pole

Captain James Cook was the first to travel cross the Antarctic Circle

Ernest Shackelton- made an attempt on the South Pole and then an attempt to cross the continent. He was made famous for his efforts in saving all of his men after they were trapped in ice.

Physical Features

Physical conditions in Antarctica are among the worst in the world. Wind speeds can reach hurricane force and have been recorded as the fastest in the world. The temperature can reach 126 degrees F. The summer is from December to February and the winter is from June to September.

The continent has ice on it that is over a mile thick at places. There are icebergs and frozen sea ice that surrounds the continent. The sea ice gets thicker in the winter time which is from June to September and thinner in the summer months from December to February. Most of the animals consist of penguins, seals, birds, and ocean life. There are no trees on the continent only small bushes and moss in parts. The growing season is extremely short with only a few months in the summer time.

Major Stations

McMurdo – United States station near the Ross Sea

Amundsen – United States station at the South Pole

Dumont – French station near the Indian Ocean

Palmer – United States station near the Weddell sea and the Southern Ocean

Vostok – Russian station in the interior of the continent

Casey – Australian station near the Indian Ocean

Davis – Australian station

History

In 1770 Captain James Cook was the first person to cross the Antarctic Circle, but he never saw land. In the 1800s several scientists, explorers, and Whalers made discoveries of Antarctica. Several countries laid claim to Antarctica. Roald Amundsen was the first to successfully reach the South Pole. Several countries have signed a treaty to help preserve the land and make it a peaceful area. Between 1,000 and 4,000 people are living in Antarctica at any given time.

Tourism is increasing every year with thousands of people visiting the continent each year. There are over 40,000 visitors each year. Most of the visitors come from the United States. There is a concern about the impact on the environment with so many tourists. Antarctica is being impacted by global warming and climate change. The whole in the Ozone Layer is getting lager

Resources

Websites:

http://www.livescience.com/21677-antarctica-facts.html

http://coolantarctica.com/

Books:

Endurance: Shackelton's Incredible Voyage by Alfred Lansing

Questions

Describe the climate of Antarctica.

Describe the human environment interaction with Antarctica.

Name some of the countries that have stations in Antarctica.

What happened to Ernest Shackelton?

How is global warming and climate change effecting Antarctica?

Problem Solving

Should companies be allowed to mine for oil and other resources in Antarctica especially with an oil shortage? How many tourists should be allowed to visit every year? Should there be a restriction on what tourists are allowed to do? How much money should be spent on research in Antarctica?

Make a list of some major concerns and challenges, then figure out a plan how to overcome those challenges.

How can countries work together to help protect Antarctica?

Activities

1. Students need to read the third book in the Dalton Brother's series and complete the study guide that goes with it.

2. Students need to read through the extra material in this workbook about Antarctica and answer the questions that go with it.

3. Students need to complete the problem solving activities.

4. Students can do further research about Antarctica and write a paper about the history, geography, or current challenges.

5. Students can work with a partner or in a group focusing either on one topic about Antarctica like the explorers or animals. The groups or partners then take the information they learned and teach another group that took a topic. Once the groups have had a chance to talk about it they can then report what they learned to the class.

6. Students can put together posters with information and pictures. Once they are completed they can share what they learned with the class.

7. Students can chose another fictional story that describes the geography of Antarctica and write a report on it.

Dalton Brothers

Book Four: Australia

Student Study Guide

Introduction

Dalton Brothers: Australia is book four in the Dalton Brother's series. It describes how the brothers finish traveling to New Zealand and Australia. They set sail on a sailboat where they head for Australia, but end up off course and land in New Zealand. In New Zealand they are able to explore the mountains and go on some hikes before they are able to fix their boat and head to Australia.

They end up going to Tasmania where they climb some mountains and then on to Australia where they have an adventure in the outback on their way to Uluru and then back to climb Mount Kosciuszko at 7,310 feet. It is the smallest mountain they have to climb, but it proves to still be a challenge for them.

The brothers then go to New Guinea to climb Duncak Jaya at 16,024 feet the tallest mountain in Oceania. It proves to be one of the toughest climbs yet. They have many more challenges on the way as they make their way closer to Mt. Everest the tallest mountain in the world.

Dalton Brothers: Australia
Chapters 1-5

1. What was their first destination after Antarctica?

2. Why are they climbing both Mt. Kosciuszko and Carstensz Pyramid?

3. What did the SERCA ship have that could help them?

4. What was the problem with the winds?

5. What did the boat hit?

6. Where did they head to when they were off course?

7. Who was Jethro?

8. How long would it take for the boat to be fixed?

9. What did they do in New Zealand while they waited for the boat to be fixed?

10. Why was Jennifer mad?

11. How did Steve Erwin die?

12. Why couldn't they relax too much in New Zealand?

13. What city did they stay in?

14. What did Josh and Jennifer do when they saw each other?

15. Why did Jennifer turn down Josh when he asked her to marry him?

16. What happened at the restaurant?

17. What is Steve's role in their travels?

18. How many miles were they going to travel in Australia?

19. What were the brother's looking forward to in Australia?

20. How were they preparing themselves?

Dalton Brothers: Australia
Chapters 6-10

1. What time did they leave New Zealand?

2. What career did Josh think Ben would be good at?

3. What is the largest city in Tasmania?

4. What was their experience like in Tasmania?

5. What was Melbourne like?

6. What was the weather like in Australia?

7. What happened to Tim?

8. Why did they have greater respect for Kosciuszko after climbing it?

9. What city did they meet Steve in?

10. What did they do in Sydney?

11. How did Ben's practical joke backfire on him?

Dalton Brothers: Australia
Chapters 11-18

1. What animals did they see in Australia?

2. Who told the brothers they would have to survive off the land?

3. Who is Jason Phillips?

4. How did they get water?

5. What animal did they hunt and eat?

6. What did they eat that tasted like chicken?

7. When did they take naps?

8. What did they find at Ulura?

9. Who thought of Uluru as a sacred place?

10. What did they do when the area got flooded?

11. What was Alex afraid of?

12. Where did they stay to get out of the water?

13. Where did they go scuba diving?

14. What did they see when they went scuba dived on the reef?

15. Who gave them money for their foundation?

16. What did Ben do to treat Alex's Jelly Fish sting?

17. What were the names of the cities in Northern Australia?

18. Where did they leave Australia?

19. What was Darwin like?

20. What prevented them from leaving Australia?

21. Who is the king of practical jokes?

22. What is Papu New Guinea like?

23. Why was Alex having World War II dreams?

24. What is the Bingham mine in Utah?

25. What does Kuwait use the money for with the oil they sell?

26. Whose birthday did they celebrate on the mountain?

27. What was the Carstensz Pyramid like?

28. What was the Java Sea like?

29. What was Singapore like?

Vocabulary

Atolls – ring-shaped islands

Lagoons – shallow pools of clear water only a few feet above sea level

Wattle – a strong, interwoven wooden framework used to build homes by early settlers in Australia

Typhoons – violent storms in the Pacific Ocean

Boomerang – a throwing stick used for hunting by Aboriginal men

Subsistence farming – growing only enough for needs of the family

Graziers – New Zealand ranchers

Copra – dried coconut meat

Marsupials – mammals whose young are raised in a pouch

Diatoms – plankton in cold ocean waters

Biographies

Nicole Kidman – Australia, famous actress

Cathrine Blanchett – Australia, famous actress

Edward Kelly – 1855 -1880 Australia, famous outlaw

King Tuheitia Paki – New Zealand Maori King

Russell Crowe – New Zealand famous actor

Hugh Jackman – Australia famous actor

Edmund Hillery – New Zealand first to climb Mt. Everest

Peter Jackson – New Zealand film director

Physical Features

The Great Dividing Range in the Eastern part of Australia is the only mountainous part of Australia. The tallest mountain on the continent is Mt. Kosciusko at 7,310 feet. The interior part of Australia is known as the bush and the outback. In the western part of Australia there is the Gibson Desert and the Great Sandy Desert. The southern part of Australia is a cooler climate and the northern part of Australia is hotter and more tropical.

New Zealand consists of two main Islands with the South Island being mountainous and the North Island being the most populous. Mt. Cook is the tallest mountain at 12,349 feet. Many of the other islands in this region of the world are tropical in nature being relatively flat and low lying. New Guinea is North of Australia with Mt. Wilhelm at 14,762 feet being the tallest mountain.

Major Cities

Canberra – capitol of Australia, in the East

Sydney – most populated city in Australia along east coast, well known for the opera house

Melbourne – large city in southern Australia

Perth – large city in western Australia

Wellington – capitol of New Zealand on the North Island

Auckland – largest city in New Zealand on the North Island

Christchurch – largest city in South Island New Zealand

History

The Aborigines of Australia and Maori of New Zealand were the original inhabitants. They lived primarily nomadic lifestyles in a clan system. The Maori are a Polynesian culture with links to the ocean and trade with other islands. The Maori also had a system of kings, while the Aborigines did not have any formal government. Both cultures have had a rich spiritual tradition tied to the land. The Aborigines were treated poorly and even hunted down by colonists, and not recognized as citizens for a long time. They were denied rights and persecuted. Today they have more rights, but are still persecuted. The Maori have done better, but still struggled to have equality in New Zealand.

European settlement started in 1788 with Australia being used as a penal colony for criminals. Farming and ranching started up by the 1850s. Australia and New Zealand were both part of the British Empire. They won their independence in the early 1900s peacefully. The European settlers quickly took over the area and controlled the government.

Resources

Websites:

https://www.cia.gov/library/publications/the-world-factbook/geos/as.html

https://www.cia.gov/library/publications/the-world-factbook/geos/nz.html

Books:

Pilkington, Doris and Nugi Garimara Follow the Rabbit Proof Fence, University of Queensland Press 2013.

Movies:

Rabbit Proof Fence: Miramax 2002

Questions

Describe the climate of Australia and New Zealand.

Describe the human environment interaction in Australia and New Zealand.

Describe how the Aborigines and Maori lived.

What is happening to the Great Barrier Reef?

Name some of the major cities in this region.

Problem Solving

Should the Aborigines and Maori have control over natural regions? How can Australia and New Zealand help the Aborigines and Maori people? How can Australia and New Zealand help protect their environment?

Make a list of some major concerns and challenges, then figure out a plan how to overcome those challenges.

How can countries work together to help protect places like the Great Barrier Reef?

Activities

1. Students need to read the forth book in the Dalton Brother's series and complete the study guide that goes with it.

2. Students need to read through the extra material in this workbook about Australia and New Zealand then answer the questions that go with it.

3. Students need to complete the problem solving activities.

4. Students can do further research about Australia and New Zealand then write a paper about the history, geography, or current challenges.

5. Students can work with a partner or in a group focusing either on one topic about Australia and New Zealand like the animals or the people. The groups or partners then take the information they learned and teach another group that took a topic. Once the groups have had a chance to talk about it they can then report what they learned to the class.

6. Students can put together posters with information and pictures. Once they are completed they can share what they learned with the class.

7. Students can chose another fictional story that describes the geography of Australia and New Zealand then write a report on it.

Dalton Brothers

Book Five: Everest

Student Study Guide

Introduction

Dalton Brothers: Everest is book five in the Dalton Brother's series. It sets the stage for the brothers to go through Thailand and into India where they meet a lot of people and go through several challenges. The brothers travel to the base camp of Everest.

The brothers meet one of their greatest challenges as they prepare themselves to climb the world's tallest mountain.

Dalton Brothers: Everest
Chapters 1-5

1. Why were they worried about being in port in Singapore?

2. Why does Josh like the diversity of weather?

3. Who thought he was agoraphobic?

4. What did Josh want to see in Cambodia?

5. Why are countries like Vietnam, Russia, and China encouraging tourism?

6. How are children getting killed in these countries?

7. What class did Alex get a C out of?

8. What did Alex want to do with his life?

9. Who is a deep sleeper?

10. What was strange about the fishing boat they saw?

11. Why were the Thai ships interested in them?

12. Why did the Dalton brothers get in trouble in Thailand?

13. How much money did the policeman want to let them go?

14. How did they get free from the police?

15. What did they do after getting free from the police?

16. What did Jennifer hate about Josh?

17. What religion dominates Thailand?

18. What did the brother's see in Thailand?

19. How did they leave Bangkok?

20. What happened to Alex?

Dalton Brothers: Everest
Chapters 6-10

1. How long was Alex in the hospital?

2. What did Ben like the most about Thailand?

3. What happened to the crew of The Endurance?

4. What did they do for Brian?

5. What did Alex need to do for them to continue their journey?

6. Why was Ben having a hard time riding his bike?

7. How did Ben solve his problem riding his bike?

8. What does the king of Thailand do?

9.   What did Ben try to drink at dinner?

10. Where have Ben Climbed?

11. What happened to Alex when he tried to go to fast on his bike?

12. What is Myanmar like?

13. How did Alex get his education?

14. What is Bangladesh like?

15. What is the main religion in Bangladesh?

16. What major rivers go through Bangladesh?

17. What city were the brothers going to in Bangladesh?

18. Who took the Dalton Brothers prisoner?

19. How did they escape?

Dalton Brothers: Everest
Chapters 11-17

1. Why did they want to stay away from strange women?

2. What form of transportation did they take in Dhaka?

3. What did they eat at Dhaka?

4. Why did the waiter want Alex to eat with his right hand?

5. What did Josh do when he entered the mosque?

6. When did Alex take off his castes?

7. What did they eat at an Indian restaurant?

8. What are some beliefs people have in India?

9. What is Dharma?

10. What city did they stay at before going to Nepal?

11. Who are Beth and Lorie?

12. What street performers did they see?

13. Who did Alex meet on the street?

14. What is the tradition in India about marriage?

15. What was Chadna's story?

16. Why did they need to be careful camping?

17. Why did they need to climb Mt. Everest in May?

18. What has happened to Nepal's government?

19. What religions are represented in Nepal?

20. What is Katmandu like?

21. Why did Ben give the authority to josh to plan the Everest climb?

22. How does Jason and Jennifer get to base camp?

23. How many miles did the Dalton brothers hike to get to base camp?

24. Why did they stop at a Buddhist monastery?

25. Who were the Sherpas?

26. What is the most dangerous part of the Everest climb?

27. Who was the lead Sherpa?

28. What did it mean when Jennifer said yes to Josh over the radio?

29. Describe Ben's dream he had about climbing Mt. Everest?

30. Who was the first to reach the top?

31. Why did Chahna go with them?

32. Who did Chahna like the most?

33. What did josh write about in his journal?

Vocabulary

Subcontinent – large landmass connected to a continent

Himalaya – highest mountain range in the world

Khyber Pass – mountain pass between India and Pakistan

Ganges River – important river in South Asia flowing East from the Himalaya, considered sacred for Hindus

Brahmaputra River – main river that flows through India and Bangladesh

Tsunami – a large wave that is caused by an underwater earthquake

Monsoons – seasonal winds that bring rain to South Asia

Guru – Indian spiritual teacher

Dharma – moral duty

Reincarnation – being born again into a different form of life

Karma – a person's actions

Biographies

Queen Sirikit – Queen of Thailand who has helped to promote the health and economy of the people of Thailand

King Chulalongkorn (Rama V) – King of Thailand who abolished slavery, and helped to modernize Thailand

Mahatma Gandhi (Mohandas Karamchand Gandhi) – social reform leader in India who promoted non-violent resistance

Jawaharlal Nehru – first prime minister of modern India

Aishwarya Rai – actress from India

Physical Features

Thailand is dominated by a tropical climate with tropical rain forests. All of South Asia is impacted by monsoons each year. These seasonal winds bring moisture from the Indian Ocean dumping in some places over a hundred inches of rain. The Gangetic Plain is a low plain area with the Ganges River it is home to millions of people in Indian and Bangladesh. Most of the Indian Subcontinent is within the tropics and is very warm year round.

The western area of South Asia is very dry with the Thar Desert. It is where the country of Pakistan is. The Himalaya is the highest mountain range in the world including some of the tallest mountains in the world. Mt. Everest is the tallest in the Himalaya.

Major Cities

Dhaka – capital of Bangladesh

New Delhi – capital of India

Katmandu – capital of Nepal

Nay Pyi Taw – capital of Myanmar

Bangkok – capital of Thailand

History

The history of South Asia is one of turmoil. Hundreds of years ago Persian invaders came into India to rule. Taj Mahal was built at this time period by a Mughal Emperor Shah Jahan in memory of his third wife who died giving birth. The British under the East India Company controlled South Asia until the end of World War II when the control went to the Indians, with Gandhi leading the non-violence resistance movement.

Mt. Everest was one of the last mountains on Earth to have been climbed. There were several failed attempts until Edmond Hillary from New Zealand was able to climb it with Sherpa Tensing Norgay. There have been over 100 people who have died attempting to climb Everest and several who have been able to climb it including Eric Weihenmayer the first blind person to have climbed Everest.

Resources

Websites:

http://www.touchthetop.com/

http://www.everestnews.com/

http://www.everestpeaceproject.org/

Books:

Weihenmayer, Erik Touch The Top of the World. Penguin Group 2002

Hillary, Edmund High Adventure: The true story of the first ascent of Everest, Oxford University Press 2003

Gandhi, Mohandas The Essential Gandhi: An anthology of his writings on his life, work, and ideas, Knopf Doubleday Publishing Group 2002

Movies:

Touch the Top of the World, Sony Pictures 2006

Everest Miramax 1998

Gandhi Sony Pictures 1982

Questions

Describe the climate of South Asia.

Describe the human environment interaction in South Asia and on Mt. Everest.

Describe how people go about climbing Mt. Everest.

What is happening with social traditions in India?

Name some of the major cities in this region.

Problem Solving

Should the countries of South Asia work together to protect the environment in the area? How can the countries of South Asia help improve social conditions of the people who live there? How can people help protect Mt. Everest?

Make a list of some major concerns and challenges, then figure out a plan how to overcome those challenges.

How can countries work together to help protect places like Mt. Everest?

Activities

1. Students need to read the fifth book in the Dalton Brother's series and complete the study guide that goes with it.

2. Students need to read through the extra material in this workbook about South Asia and Mt. Everest then answer the questions that go with it.

3. Students need to complete the problem solving activities.

4. Students can do further research about South Asia and Mt. Everest then write a paper about the history, geography, or current challenges.

5. Students can work with a partner or in a group focusing either on one topic about South Asia and Mt. Everest like the animals, climbers, or the people. The groups or partners then take the information they learned and teach another group that took a topic. Once the groups have had a chance to talk about it they can then report what they learned to the class.

6. Students can put together posters with information and pictures. Once they are completed they can share what they learned with the class.

7. Students can chose another fictional story that describes the geography of South Asia and Mt. Everest then write a report on it.

Dalton Brothers

Book Six: Europe

Student Study Guide

Introduction

Dalton Brothers: Europe is book six in the Dalton Brother's series. It sets the stage for the brothers to go through Europe and into North Africa where they meet a lot of people and go through several challenges. The brothers face their greatest challenges yet.

The brothers meet one of their greatest challenges as they prepare themselves to climb Mont Blanc in France at 15,782 feet and Mount Elbrus at 18,510 feet located in the Caucus Mountains of Russia.

Dalton Brothers: Europe
Chapters 1-5

1. Who was waiting for them in Katmandu?

2. What challenge did they have to solve?

3. Who was Alex having feelings for?

4. What are Alex's beliefs?

5. What might the Russians and Chinese think about the brothers?

6. What would happen to Chahna if they can't help her?

7. Describe the city of Lucknow.

8. What was their hotel like?

9. What was Ben thinking about in Lucknow?

10. What did Mother Teresa do?

11. What was the weather like?

12. Why were they camping alongside the road?

13. What are some challenges of overpopulation?

14. Describe the River Ganges.

15. What was happening to Josh?

16. Why did a boy follow them?

17. What sport did they see people watching in a stadium?

18. How might the money they receive for the Tabby Foundation help the children of India?

19. Where did they experience flooding?

20. What was it like traveling on the road to Tibet?

21. Describe what happened to the Dali Lama?

22. Why where they going door-to-door?

Dalton Brothers: Europe
Chapters 6-10

1. What was the Chinese boarder like?

2. Where were they going to meet the SERCA team?

3. Why did the Chinese soldier believe they were American spies?

4. What was Ben thinking about after the soldiers took them?

5. What was Josh's advice when they were in jail?

6. Why didn't they leave Chahna in an orphanage?

7. How did they get Chahna out of India?

8. What has been the relationship between Russia and the United States?

9. Who is Dmitry?

10. What did the Dalton brother's go through in jail?

11. How did they get out of jail?

12. Why were they excited about leaving China?

13. Why did Dmitry ride with the Dalton brothers through China?

14. What is the Taiga?

15. What part of Russia were they traveling through?

16. Describe Lake Baikal.

17. What desert did they travel through?

18. How were the brothers tested by Dmitry?

Dalton Brothers: Europe
Chapters 11-17

1. What is the Gobi Desert like?

2. What did Josh think about Dmitry?

3. Describe Mongolia.

4. What did Josh do at the Gandan Monastery?

5. What did Dmitry do with his family?

6. What lakes did Ben skip rocks on in Russia and in Utah?

7. What was the forest like?

8. What is Irkutsk like?

9. What was Russia like after the collapse of communism?

10. What does Dmitry do to help Siberian tigers?

11. How do they prepare for the bears?

12. What animal did they follow?

13. What was Norisk like?

14. What did they want to avoid on their way to the North Pole?

15. How did they get to the North Pole?

16. What was the name of their boat?

17. What happened when they saw Fairbanks, Alaska?

18. Where were they going to go on their way through Europe?

19. How did they get to Europe?

20. What did they do in Iceland?

21. What did they do in Scotland?

22. Where did they spend Christmas and New Years?

23. Where were Josh and Jennifer going to get married?

24. Why where they going to climb Mt. Elbrus?

25. What did Josh write in his journal?

Vocabulary

Loess - a rich soil left by glaciers (found throughout Northern Europe)

Dikes – large mounds of dirt to hold by the sea (found in the Netherlands)

Fjords – steep sided inlets from the sea created by glaciers (found in Scandinavia)

Mistral – strong northern wind from the Alps

Siroccos – hot dry winds from North Africa

Feudalism – a system of government where nobles and monarchs pledged loyalty with each other in exchange for land

Reformation – religious movement with the intent of reforming religious thought in Europe

European Union – political organization in Europe with the goal to have a unified economic system

Biographies

Leonardo daVinci 1452 – 1519 famous artist and inventor

Michelangelo 1475 – 1564 famous artist

William Shakespeare 1564 – 1616 famous playwright, poet, actor

Isaac Newton 1642 – 1727 physicist mathematician

J.K. Rowling 1965 – author (Harry Potter)

Physical Features

The Scandinavian countries are the northern most countries in Europe. They go into the Arctic Circle. Norway, Sweden, and Finland have long cold winters and short cool summers. Iceland is an island country covered by glaciers and volcanoes. Ireland known as the emerald island has a temperate climate. The United Kingdom including Scotland, Wales, and Northern Ireland is a set of islands with a temperate climate and highlands in the north in Scotland with several mountains.

The main part of Europe is a large peninsula with the Northern European Plain in the North a flat area where there are a lot of farms. The Netherlands is flat with many areas below sea level kept dry with dikes and pumps. The Alps is a mountain chain in the center of Europe. They are tall rugged mountains noted for their beauty. Switzerland is surrounded by the Alps. The Alps can also be found in Germany, France, Italy, and Austria. The Pyrenees Mountains are on the boarder of France and Spain.

Southern Europe is influenced by the Mediterranean Sea. The climate named after the Mediterranean has mild winters, is dry most of the year, and has moderate temperatures in the summer. Southern Europe is a great vacation spot for many Europeans like Southern California is too many Americans.

Major Cities

Dublin – capitol of Ireland

London – capitol of the United Kingdom

Paris – capitol of France

Rome – capitol of Italy

Athens – capitol of Greece

Berlin – capitol of Germany

History

Europe has been the birthplace of much of modern society including science, art, and politics. The early civilizations came from the city states of Greece including Athens and Sparta. Alexander the Great spread Greek influence into Egypt and India. Rome conquered most of what is now Europe. There is still Greek and Roman influence in Europe and in the world. Europe quickly fell into a feudal system with monarchs throughout the countries. For hundreds of years it was the Catholic Church and the monarchs who had power in Europe.

It was the Enlightenment, Reformation, and Renaissance that brought about dramatic change in Europe in scientific thought, politics, and religion. The age of exploration brought European ideas throughout the world including Africa, the New World, and Asia. Feudalism and a lot of European traditions came crashing to an end during World War I giving way to communistic ideas. World War II hit Europe hard forcing many of the countries to give up on their empires and to rethink old traditions.

Europe since World War II has tried to stay out of most world conflicts. The United Nations was established, and the European Union was formed. Now Europe is a continent with a lot of immigrants coming to find a better life. There are a lot of challenges facing Europe today including economy, social programs, and the environment. Most of the countries have a social system where there are a lot of governmental programs.

Resources

Websites:

http://europa.eu/index_en.htm

Books:

Movies:

Questions

Describe the climate of Europe.

Describe the human environment interaction in Europe.

Describe how people in Europe get along with each other.

What is happening with the European Union?

Name some of the major cities in this region.

Problem Solving

Should the countries of Europe work together to protect the environment in the area? How can the countries of Europe help improve social conditions of the people who live there? How can people help protect the environment in Europe?

Make a list of some major concerns and challenges, then figure out a plan how to overcome those challenges.

How can countries work together to help protect places in Europe?

Activities

1. Students need to read the sixth book in the Dalton Brother's series and complete the study guide that goes with it.

2. Students need to read through the extra material in this workbook about Europe then answer the questions that go with it.

3. Students need to complete the problem solving activities.

4. Students can do further research about Europe then write a paper about the history, geography, or current challenges.

5. Students can work with a partner or in a group focusing either on one topic about Europe like the animals, climbers, or the people. The groups or partners then take the information they learned and teach another group that took a topic. Once the groups have had a chance to talk about it they can then report what they learned to the class.

6. Students can put together posters with information and pictures. Once they are completed they can share what they learned with the class.

7. Students can chose another fictional story that describes the geography of Europe then write a report on it.

Dalton Brothers

Book Seven: Kilimanjaro

Student Study Guide

Introduction

Dalton Brothers: Kilimanjaro is book seven and final in the Dalton Brother's series. It details the journey of the brothers in Africa and up Kilimanjaro. The book wraps up the personal relationship with the brothers and other characters in the series. The book is to help students gain a greater knowledge and understanding about Africa. Students can explore many different areas of Africa including Northern Africa, Sub-Saharan Africa, and the Middle East.

Africa has a lot of rich cultures with several common threads such as Islam, native tribes, and a strong connection to the environment.

Dalton Brothers: Kilimanjaro
Chapters 1-5

1. What trapped the Dalton brothers on the mountain?

2. What can happen at 17,000 feet?

3. How were they prepared for an avalanche?

4. What happened when they were caught in an avalanche?

5. What happened to Alex?

6. How did they get Alex off the mountain?

7. What did they feel like in the hospital?

8. What did Ben do for Alex?

9. Why does Ben want Alex to climb Mt. Kilimanjaro?

10. What was Ben's plan in the hospital?

11. How did Ben change from when he was in Paris?

12. Where were Josh and Jennifer going to get married?

13. What was Alex's decision about climbing Mt. Kilimanjaro?

14. Why did Alex want to get out of the hospital?

15. How did the mountains change for Alex?

16. What language did a little girl speak to Alex?

17. Why were the people giving Alex flowers?

18. How did Alex feel when he rode his bike again?

19. Where will Josh and Jennifer go on their honeymoon?

20. Who did Alex miss?

21. What is the country of Turkey like?

22. What was the joke about Batman?

23. What is Batman like?

24. What are some of the strange cities in the United States?

25. What happened to Josh when he went running in the morning?

26. What is Turkey like?

27. What did they see in Gaziantep?

28. What happened to Alex's leg?

29. What was Alex feeling about climbing Kilimanjaro?

Dalton Brothers: Kilimanjaro
Chapters 6-10

1. Why did Ben want to get past Syria and Israel?

2. What would make the brothers suspicious looking?

3. Why does Josh want to see Jerusalem?

4. What is in Egypt they want to see?

5. What did they hear when they left Damascus?

6. When did Israel become a country?

7. What were some of the sights they saw in Jerusalem?

8. Why were they worried about the Gaza Strip?

9. What did they discover in the hospital that gave them hope of peace?

10. What is Cairo like?

11. Why is the Nile River important?

12. What was the weather like in Egypt?

13. What did Josh fear about the heat?

14. Who is Ahziz?

15. What was Jennifer afraid of?

16. How did they travel down the Nile River?

17. What did they do when they visited the pyramids?

18. What did Ben do in the Nile River?

Dalton Brothers: Kilimanjaro
Chapters 11-17

1. What was at Karnack?

2. What was Sudan like?

3. Why did children come to see them?

4. What were the children from the village like?

5. What is Khartoum like?

6. What is Mullah?

7. What was Ahziz hiding from them?

8. Why did the CIA get involved?

9. What animals did they have to worry about in the Nile River?

10. What is Lake Victoria like?

11. What is the Serengeti?

12. What is the Great Rift Valley?

13. What animals did they see?

14. What were the risks of climbing Mt. Kilimanjaro?

15. What is Kilimanjaro like?

16. How did Jennifer and Josh's wedding turn out?

17. What was happening to Josh?

18. How did they feel when they reached the top?

19. What did Josh write in hid journal?

Vocabulary

Wadis – dry riverbeds made by storms

Oasis – a place in the desert where water comes to the surface

Bedouin – people who migrate from the deserts of Southwest Asia to North Africa to trade objects

Suez Canal – a canal that connects the Red Sea to the Mediterranean Sea

Desalination – the process of removing salt from sea water

Desertification – the process of turning land into a desert after prolonged periods of drought

Savanna – grasslands with scattered trees

Apartheid – government policy of separation of races in South Africa

Poaching – illegal hunting

Biographies

Nelson Mandela was the first black South African president who was imprisoned for more than twenty years for speaking out against the government.

Saddam Hussein was the dictatorial leader of Iraq who killing many of his own people and started a war with his neighbors Iran and Kuwait. He was executed for his crimes by his people.

Osama Bin Laden was a terrorist leader who planned out several terrorist attacks around the world. He was killed on a raid by the United States military.

Physical Features

In this region of the world there are many extremes from desert to mountain. In North Africa the weather is Mediterranean and desert. The largest desert in the world dominates Northern Africa. The Sahara continues to grow a few inches every year. The Nile River is the longest river in the world over three thousand miles long. It is the only source of water for several countries in North Africa.

The Atlas Mountains run across North Africa going through the country of Morocco. Mt. Kilimanjaro is the tallest mountain in Africa. It is a volcano and sits near the equator. There is tropical rainforest near the equator.

The Serengeti is an area in Tanzania where there are a lot of wild animals. It is a rich grassland that supports a wide variety of animals. Many people go on safaris in the Serengeti to see the animals. The Great Rift Valley is an area in Eastern Africa that is splitting apart with faults forming a rift valley. It is home to a lot of different kinds of animals.

Lake Victoria is the largest lake in Africa. The Nile river flows into the lake. Victoria Falls is the largest falls in Africa and is much larger than Niagara Falls in the United States.

Major Cities

Damascus – capitol of Syria

Jerusalem – Capitol of Israel

Cairo – Capitol of Egypt

Khartoum – Capitol of Sudan

History

The history of this region of the world goes back to the beginning of civilizations. Ancient Egypt with its pharaohs and pyramid building was the breadbasket of the region for the people in the area. Mesopotamia was the home to Babylon and many other large civilizations at the center of the Tigress and Euphrates rivers.

This is also home to Jerusalem mentioned in the Bible, Torah, and Koran as one of the holiest cities in the world. The rich history is home to three major religions; Christianity, Islam, and Judaism. It is the source of a lot of unrest and tension in the region with Muslims and Jews fighting each other.

Africa south of the Sahara is known for the slave trade and kingdoms that promoted trade to Europeans and the East. When the age of discovery commenced it was Africa first to be conquered and pillaged by European nations who took over tribal areas and organized them into nations. After World War II many of these European controlled nations gained their independence only to collapse into civil war and chaos. Since then many of these countries have fought for freedoms and equality among different ethnic groups for power in their respective governments.

Today many of the countries of Africa face poverty, disease, and violence. Countries are struggling to survive with many challenges including the threat to forests, animals, and the environment from its inhabitants.

Resources

Websites:

http://www.africa.com/

Books:

An Ordinary Man by Paul Rusesabagina

Left to Tell by Immaculee Illibagiza

A Long Way Gone: Memoirs of a boy Soldier by Ishmael Beah

Movies:

Mysteries of the Nile, IMAX film

Hotel Rwanda

Mandela

Questions

Describe the climate of Africa.

Describe the human environment interaction in Africa.

Describe how people in Africa get along with each other.

What is happening with diseases in Africa?

Name some of the major cities in this region.

Problem Solving

Should the countries of Africa work together to protect the environment in the area? How can the countries of Africa help improve social conditions of the people who live there? How can people help protect the environment in Africa?

Make a list of some major concerns and challenges, then figure out a plan how to overcome those challenges.

How can countries work together to help protect places in Africa?

Activities

1. Students need to read the seventh book in the Dalton Brother's series and complete the study guide that goes with it.

2. Students need to read through the extra material in this workbook about Africa then answer the questions that go with it.

3. Students need to complete the problem solving activities.

4. Students can do further research about Africa then write a paper about the history, geography, or current challenges.

5. Students can work with a partner or in a group focusing either on one topic about Africa like the animals, climbers, or the people. The groups or partners then take the information they learned and teach another group that took a topic. Once the groups have had a chance to talk about it they can then report what they learned to the class.

6. Students can put together posters with information and pictures. Once they are completed they can share what they learned with the class.

7. Students can chose another fictional story that describes the geography of Africa then write a report on it.

www.ingramcontent.com/pod-product-compliance
Lightning Source LLC
Chambersburg PA
CBHW081218280526

45787CB00006B/2437